A JOURNEY OF ASKING, SEEKING,
AND KNOCKING

AS I WALK *in the* HEART OF *God*

TERRY BUHECKER

ASPIRE
PUBLISHING HUB LLC.

Library of Congress Control Number: 2025916719

ISBN
979-8-89683-149-5 (Paperback)
979-8-89683-150-1 (eBook)
979-8-89683-148-8 (Hardcover)

To everyone who has read my thoughts and poems (many written in the rhythm of my heart, not in the laws of poetry) and urged me to share, that I should publish them in a book.

And to my daughter, who asked me if she could have my notebooks. Let it be known that when I die, they go to her.

TABLE OF CONTENTS

Acknowledgments ix

Introduction xi

The Beginning 1

The Lamb 3

Fear of the Lord 4

Master of All Things 5

Be Not Silent..6

Walk with Me 7

Dear Father 8

A Little Strength 9

The Hand of God 10

Dear Lord 11

The Calm..12

God's Foundation of His Wall...............................13

It's Too Much..15

Our First Love...16

Now I Get On..17

The Light of Life...18

Friendship 19

When Will I Believe Enough? 20

What More Can I Do? 21

I Made It Through Today! 22

His Soul Can Hold Me 23

God's Hand 24

What Am I Thankful for Today? 25

Willingness 27

Cuddly................................28

Forgiveness................................29

Be My Vision 30

One More Step................................31

Prayer for me................................32

Fruit Trees................................33

The Tree in the Vineyard 36

Noisy 37

Trust Me................................38

The Bride and the Groom 39

Robert's Letter................................40

Am I Begging at the Gate? 41

Wait on the Lord................................42

About the Author................................45

AS I WALK IN THE HEART OF GOD:
A Journey of Asking, Seeking, and Knocking

*The words and thoughts given by
my friend, The Lord Jesus*

Terry Buhecker

Acknowledgments

I am thankful for the moving of the Spirit, who has shown me the estate of my heart and the loving care of my Lord and his Father, who in mercy spoke to my heart and still searches the earth for souls.

Who are searching for love and are crying to the Father, Son, and Holy Ghost.

It is the whispers of God's voice to my heart that give me such thoughts, as I write them down they feed my soul and inspire me to share them with others.

In the last days, there will not be a famine as men
know famine but there will be a famine of hearing.
(Amos 8:11)

None the less when the Son of man comes
back, will he find faith on the earth?
(Luke 18:8)

It is so easy to fill our days with the endless chatter of the world. There is another verse that can explain this as well:

Hell and death are never full because the
eyes of man are never satisfied.
(Proverbs 27:20)

If it were not for the whispers of God's voice to my heart, these thoughts, poems, and inspirations would not be possible.

If anything, I pray that this will point to the one who gave his life for all.

There was a time when I did not know him, but I felt him… in my heart.

Yet one day in desperation I cried out to my God, and he heard my prayer. "Dear Lord, teach me to be like Jesus. He is the only one who knows the way back to heaven."

It was a powerful prayer; I thought my heart would jump out of my chest. This journey of learning and loving his Son Jesus has just started. It will take an eternity to discover the heart of the Lord who gave himself for me.

He loves me!

Introduction

This book is not about me, and yet I am intertwined in its pages. So I am going to give you a little background about myself. Perhaps the best way to view it is that it is "my testimony," of how my Lord sought me for many years before I turned around and sought him.

I visited with death before I was born; anyway, that is how I see it. My mother would tell me a story of how she rolled a pickup truck down a steep embankment in a canyon long ago. It rolled over and over and over and over—many times, according to her. My aunt and my oldest brother were also in the truck with her when it went out of control and down the embankment. When it finally stopped, there was a big boulder in the truck as well. She would tell me how the boulder was tumbling around in the cab of the truck. She would always say, "No one was hurt," like it was a miracle to even be alive, let alone not be hurt. Then she'd finish the story by saying, "And I was pregnant with you."

I had a nightmare, the same nightmare that occurred over and over and over (I'm leaving a few *overs* out). I was in total darkness, in a cage. I was so scared I could not move, and yet I was pacing back and forth, like a caged lion you see at the zoo. The darkness was so black I would fight it because if I didn't, I would die, as if it was coming back to claim what it was cheated from. My first remembrance of this nightmare was well before the age of seven. I slept in my crib until I was seven years old.

On my seventh birthday, my parents gave me a grown-up bed. I was very petite.

I had this very same nightmare well into my twenties. By then it started to come every night, and I was afraid to go to bed. I was afraid to go to sleep since I was afraid I would not wake up. That is when I truly started to cry out to the Lord Jesus, except it was more like saying his name over and over, struggling to wake up before I died.

I was married with two young children, and Jesus was my only hope to save me from the darkness that came every night for my soul. I am quite sure that was my experience when my mother rolled her pickup.

When I was a young girl, my dad would take me to church. One Sunday he forgot me after church was over. I got lost in the crowd in a very big church, and I wandered off to a part that no one was in. Soon as I was wandering, no one was anywhere. I wasn't scared; it seemed to me in my heart that God was there. The sun was streaming through the window, and everything was peaceful. There was a janitor there, and I was finally found. I can still remember the disgusted look on his face as he asked me for Dad's name. He asked me what our phone number was and called my home for someone to come get me. Back in the day, when you had to dial the phone, it was easy to know your phone number. At a young age, that is all I remember. Who picked me up? Mom or Dad, I cannot say. If the house was angry or happy when I came home, I cannot say. I am thankful for the exposure to the Bible stories of our Lord Jesus at a young age. Some were confusing, and I pondered them in my heart, like, *Why would Jesus cleanse the temple?*

Life got a little more complicated; Mom and Dad got divorced. There were the usual battles: Dad did not want to give Mom money, and Mom did not live in the same town with

Dad. I am not sure how everything came about, but we ended up living with Dad, who was gone most of the time. He worked long hours and found a girlfriend. Mom had a boyfriend. Both of them got remarried and started to build a new life. It didn't seem like we fit in anywhere. Not with Dad nor with Mom. But the Lord? He was there.

I started paying tithing. There was a man, the treasurer, who would take people's tithing and then type them a receipt (good proof for taxes that you paid). There would always be a line. I was very shy and didn't want anyone to know that I was going to tithe, so I would wait until everyone was gone, and I would walk up to the counter I could hardly see over and give the man a quarter. He would type a receipt for a quarter. He never smiled at such a childish gesture, he treated me like I had given one hundred dollars. You could buy a lot of candy with a quarter in those days. That stern face was actually very kind to me.

At twelve, I moved in with my mom and stepdad. They had a new baby boy, my brother. My dad was very disappointed in me; he let me know that I was not welcome to move back with him. I lost hold of the Lord in those trying teenage years. I tried to read the Bible, but I just couldn't get past Mathew chapter 1, so I set God aside. I stopped going to church. No one in Mom's house went to church. Instead I tried to find some love and security in a world that so far hadn't offered too much.

At seventeen, I left home (a big mistake) to take care of myself. I ended up marrying a man who ached in his heart as much as I did. It was not a good marriage. He always worked for sure, but he drank most of his wages. I would carry big black garbage bags of beer cans out of the house every day. People would come over and drink with him and watch TV. Not exactly the loving home I was trying to create for two children that I had brought into the world. I was lonely, so I started reading my Bible, and oddly enough, the first time I opened it, the first thing I read was Proverbs 23:29-35 (KJV):

Who hath woe? who hath sorrow? who hath con-
tentions? who hath babbling? who hath wounds
without cause? who hath redness of eyes?

They that tarry long at the wine; they
that go to seek mixed wine.

Look not thou upon the wine when it is red, when it giveth
his colour in the cup, when it moveth itself aright.

At the last it biteth like a serpent, and stingeth like an adder.

Thine eyes shall behold strange women, and
thine heart shall utter perverse things.

Yea, thou shalt be as he that lieth down in the midst of
the sea, or as he that lieth upon the top of a mast.

They have stricken me, shalt thou say, and I was
not sick; they have beaten me, and I felt it not:
when shall I awake? I will seek it yet again.

Those verses hit home. They were a very accurate description of my life. I may not have been the one drinking the cup, but I was living in the despair of its effect. It was a life that made no sense; it did not have any joy in it. That message that day started a journey for me. I started looking earnestly for the Lord. On top of everything going on, the nightmare of my childhood started to come again very frequently. I was so afraid to go to bed; I would lie there crying out for the Lord to help me.

I started studying with different denominations, and one night when I was saying my prayers, my husband in disgust said to me, "You are just praying to that [I was studying with a group of people of a certain religion] religion's God." Well, when you pray to God, it's to God, not to a religious body. That started the wheels turning to seek Jesus, to seek his Father, because all I knew was Jesus is in heaven with his Father after walking here on earth. He knows the way to heaven. If you want to go to heaven, that safe haven, he is the one to follow. So I asked the Father of heaven to teach me to be like his Son Jesus so I could go to heaven too. I thought my heart would come out of my chest; it's like it leaped for joy. That prayer has forever changed my life, and now thirty-nine years later, he is still teaching me.

If it were not for the Lord, my Blessed Lord, who has comforted me and reassured me of who I Am is, now the person I was is not the same person I became, a transformation from death unto life. My thoughts here on earth, my Lord has turned to thoughts of heaven above.

So I may enter into his presence when I pray and also be in his presence as I walk hand in hand with my God throughout the day.

The Beginning

There is a peace that God and his Son gives me when I write. And my thoughts are not mine, but they are of the Spirit, who searches the deep meditations of the heart. When I enter into the message of love and hope the Lord offers me, well, it brings me peace. There is a rest in the peace of God, like the picture of a green pasture on a cool summer day with the flock, the sheep, resting at noon. A picture painted over and over again in my heart. The comfort a new day brings as the rays of the morning light shine, the birds are singing their song to the first rays of the sun, the promise of a new day. My heart cannot say that enough. Perhaps there is a reason that the Lord is letting me write these things in this book.

I am not a preacher. I am not starting a church. My Lord Jesus did not start a church. He came preaching the Kingdom of God, a Kingdom that was established before the creation of this world. The Word of this Kingdom is found in the Bible; it's found on your knees. The Spirit has taught me precious communications with the Lord; let the Spirit move through you. For his Spirit is my strength, and it is continually before the throne of God the Father and his Son, Jesus, the Prince of Peace.

Let the Lord in; he knocks at the door. He does all the work; we just have to say *yes*. *Yes* to the love of Jesus. *Yes* to letting his life shine in ours. *Yes* to faith that is a gift from God himself. *Yes.* This *yes* is for every day. It brings a freedom of love, hope, peace, and joy. It lets us have the smile of our Lord in our hearts.

I was reading the Bible, searching for answers, and I read about a Lamb, a precious Lamb that was sacrificed to save the world. It was very disturbing because I did not know about this Lamb. In all the years that I went to "church" as a child, I never heard about a Lamb. I knew Jesus died on the cross; you see pictures everywhere. Then as I pondered about this mystery, a little whisper to my heart: "It is Jesus."

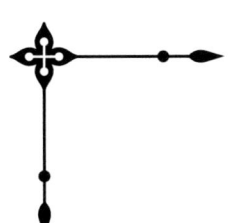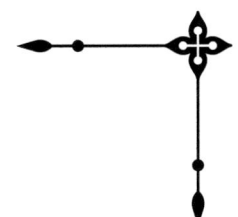

The Lamb

Who is the Lord? That I may believe on him?
Who is the Lamb?
The one who gave his life a sacrifice…
For my sin?
The one who beats in my breast?
The one who came and lets me rest safe within the fold.
Who does not meet me with the just reward for my sin.
But instead, his hand stretched out—
It lifts me up—
He carries my burden—
And has already paid the price
With his life—My Lord, the Son of God.

Jesus, what part of my burden am I not giving thee?

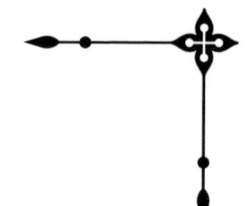

Fear of the Lord

If you are afraid of Jesus
Let him in the boat.
Because once he is in the boat:
The storm will cease
Water will be calm
You will instantly be at the shore where Jesus told you to go.
Please let Jesus in the boat.

Master of All Things

Of my Heart?
My Life?
My desires?

Of the affections of my heart?
Of my home?
My small tender space?

Is the Master at the helm?

Be Not Silent

Dear Lord, I have asked many petitions—My heart
knows that you have answered them—In your own time.

Forgive me, Father, for in my weakness I get impatient.
Nothing looks like I want it to.
Nothing according to my will.

I think, "I'll do this"—it starts to smell.
"I'll do that!" I make people anguish.
No! No! Not my will but thine.

So my heart, it waits;
Waits upon the Lord.
To accomplish what is best.

For me to die in your arms.
How should I go up, my Lord?
How should I go up?

As I Walk in the Heart of God

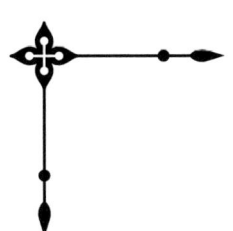
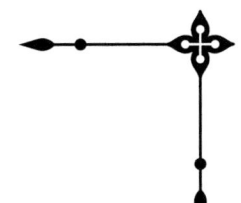

Walk with Me

He asked, "Will you walk with me?
Why do you walk alone?"
I was surprised, I did not know,
I thought I was going home.

But the way my love, My Savior, trod
Was slightly to the right.
I missed the mark, gone astray,
was wandering in the night.

His hand, it ever showed the way.
His eyes so tender in love.
My heart, it burned and jumped with joy.
As hand in hand we walked, as one, in peace above.

My Savior is my love, my guide
A covert for my heart.
So just today, please let me stand
Much closer, never more to part.

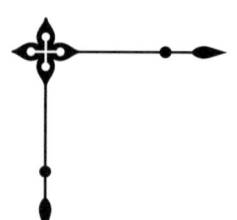

Dear Father

Thank you for bringing a calm in my life;
I did not recognize it, SAD!
I looked around, what to do?
I could not see!
I could not see!
I managed to get many things done, but were they right?
Was it what I should be doing till the setting of the sun? And
still you call, unsettled I came and you, you brought the calm.
It is just me, no purpose here;
I just wander on and on.
I just wander on.

Reflections:

_____
_____
_____
_____
_____
_____
_____

A Little Strength

A little strength—I have found in thee—a little strength
A newborn babe, it is praised, "How strong they are"
Their little head bobbing, lifting off their mother's chest.
A Little Strength

They grab your finger and hold on.
It's hard to pry it off.
Look how strong a grip they have!
A Little Strength

Soon they push on stubby legs
And fiercely hold your hands.
Look how strong! Upright they stand.
A Little Strength

God has given strength each day
To take a step with God.
A little strength from heaven above
To walk the path of Love.

The Hand of God

A comfort gives
His arms surround my soul.
I am so small and he so great
He is my all in all.

Satisfaction burns within my heart—
When my Lord draws near.
It cannot compare to anything
The world it offers here.

So why in tears do I walk each day?
Why mourn my soul of loss?
When gentle hands, they are my Lord's
They caress my tearstained face.

A victory song, to shout with joy
A victory won by love—
His Son has done the impossible
He's turned my thoughts above.

I take a step, a step in faith
Oh yes, just take another.
Keep on the path, the proven way
And we'll rejoice in that great day!

Yes, we'll rejoice together.

Dear Lord

Somehow my heart, it turns to thee
The loneliness to fill
Take away the yearnings of an empty heart
The empty bed, the lonely days, the dreams of one to come.

What do you give me in replace? The ray of light so clear.
A hand, a touch, a voice that whispers in my ear.
Please forgive the earthly thoughts that
fight the heavenly peace.
Let me not weary, my Lord; please help me to fill my place.

Reflections:

_____
_____
_____
_____
_____
_____
_____

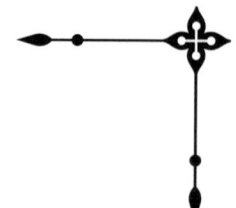

The Calm

When the Lord calms the storm—
What do I do with the churning memories?
Do I hang on to the fear of overwhelm?
Do I hear all the noise of a storm long gone?

Do I hear the voice of my Lord?
Do I ask my Lord for help to look ahead?
Do I invite him into my life?
Or do I drown in fear of a storm long gone?

Grow up, little girl—
What about the little child?
Does she die in the storm?
Does she die in memories of storms long gone?

God's Foundation of His Wall

There is a foundation in God's way.
A place to build your hope and dreams with God, in love.
A place so solid nothing can shake it—
Not even the imagination of an unruly heart.

There are walls, but where do the walls start?
A foundation—one that is not sitting on the dust and
shifting sands of our thoughts, our wavering ways, but on
the solid unchangeable, powerful, strength of God.

It does not need a man;
It does not need a woman.
We only compromise; we are weak.
Yet in the strength of the foundation, we
are made strong and useful.

In the beginning, the corner where all is measured to.
All is lined up—where the standard is set.
Our Lord—our Jesus who set the wall—proved the wall.
Who even today makes all measure to the standard of God.

I sit and listen to the powerful message of Jesus himself
who built this wall. Each layer so precious, so important.
It makes my heart full of joy—leap with wonder.
Sometimes I feel that I will burst with Love.

The wall of this house, it's God's.
The cornerstone is God's Son.

The beautiful foundation stones so
carefully shape? God's ministry.
My little place so insignificant and the wall is so great.
What love is this? That God gives me a place.

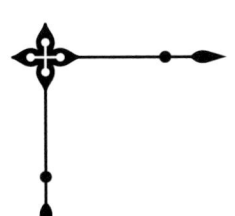
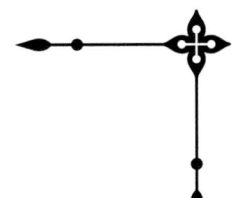

It's Too Much

I keep saying, "It's too much"—"It's too far."
"You do not need to draw near to Jesus."
"Others are so much more important."
"No, there is no need, not for me!"

But here I am, standing in the place I love to be in.
A place at the table—with the servants.
The servants of my Father. I am not
worthy—not for a morsel.
But here my cup runneth over.
Where my cup runneth over.

Our First Love

My heart the Lord has sealed forever—
An eternal bond of Love—
It's strong—
It's warm—
It's powerful—
It feels so wonderful that it seems to be made up—
But it's not—
Two souls knit together equal one—one soul—
So strong—
So close—
So comforting—

That if I say, "Your first love is the Lord"—
Then you say, "Your first love is the Lord"—
Together as one:
"Our Lord, you are our first Love"—

❧

A castle in heaven
A room in heaven
A treasure in heaven
Blessings poured out,
so mighty,
It's more than my understanding can receive.

Now I Get On

Now I get on with the needs of the day.
But now at this time I can sadly say,
That even though I read and prayed,
The thoughts of the day—
They got in the way.

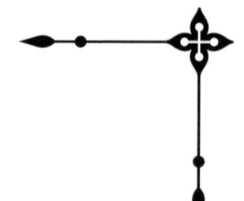

The Light of Life

The light of life
Springing forth from the Earth
A first love blooming
In the hearts of men

Created by God
From the darkness that covers
A heart void of the love of the Lord
Nothing but emptiness of want

But as the Lord our God moves
in the hearts of men
He says, "Let there be light"
And then there is

A beautiful glow
from the Son of Man
whose home is found
in the heart of man.

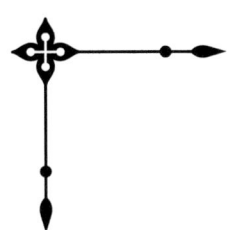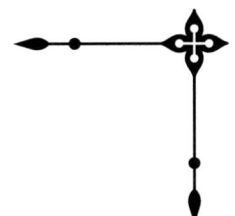

Friendship

It is made up of two words: one, *friend*, who is more than an acquaintance; and two: *ship*, a small vessel. Where all travel together in the same direction.

What is a true friend? Each carries along their own personal cares, hopes, baggage, and dreams. What if each could help the other to empty the baggage, fears, and concerns overboard? Moving along together with their hopes and dreams.

Somehow baggage seems priceless. We identify our life with it. Yet if we let go, would we disappear? Would we cease to breathe? Is the past what makes us visible for the future?

Maybe when all is clean, neat, and all the fear, anger, confusion, malice is gone, we would find:
    the air refreshing,
    the sunshine bright,
    the peace from the beauty now in our place to dwell.

And a true friend, that bond of true friendship—a delightful place to exist!

Come to ME, I will teach you about My Kingdom!

When Will I Believe Enough?

Somewhere far ahead, away off,
is the amazing place and contentment of my God.

Where we stand around the throne in total peace
contentment of what God gives when we surrender everything

He gives me a glimpse as I fall back to prey
of fleshly desires and despair of the day.

But today my Lord, the Son of my God, has lifted me up
and let joy engulf me as I tread on.

It makes me nervous to be so light of heart,
to have such victory, such peace in the storm.

Dear Lord, it is only you, the one who can give such peace
If only for the day…my heart lifted high

Can't wait for the day that this will not be taken away.
I know it's not you but me Lord, who lets my peace fall short.
As the imagination of a wicked old heart that wants
The old cloth, the old wine bottle, to whimper and whine

But you, my Lord, my King, and my Love
Divine…You gave your life to give me
The new garment, the new vessel for the new wine

That will not burst.

What More Can I Do?

I say this with only one thought, that there is something I
can do to bring about a miracle in my life. How FOOLISH.
I have no power, no ability. I cry to God and His Son, but
only because I want him to bring about this miracle.

My intentions are misplaced.

Like I could catch God in a trap to do
my will—how foolish is that.

I Made It Through Today!

Teach us, Lord, our days to number.
We only need to count to one
One day—one day—one day
For each day is one day.

How can I let one day slip?
It may be the only day left.
Where God reveals his Son, His Word, His Light
How can I make up one day I miss? It's forever gone.

One chance to read, one meeting to go to,
One chance to be a light, just one
One day to do it all,
Just one day.

One more day to learn contentment,
One more day to accept the counsel of God,
One more day of Strength,
Wisdom to love God.

One more day of Peace,
That passes the understanding of men,
One more day to spend in communion with my God,
The God of Heaven.

His Soul Can Hold Me

Where is true love?
My Lord Jesus gave all, true love for my soul.
But if he is far away.
Will I know his love?
Will I look to my Lord for comfort and hope?

So many times when I think of love, its companionship.
Two people together,
Those tender moments, where you forget the storm.
It makes you look to the man,
to find that one to hold and cherish you.

But, Lord, when I have put that aside,
And I seek thee, Dear Father, my hope, my love, my comfort.
When I look to thee, I have found that your spirit, your love,
and your purpose for me,
Dear Lord, Your soul it comforts me.
It holds me, it quiets the wild storm of the heart
To bring me to you in eternity
and directs me.
To feed on the peace of heaven.

In joy, laughing, singing in your presence.
Speaking my desires to you as you listen to me.
Listening to you as you hold, comfort, and direct me.
Yes, Lord, you hold, you enfold my soul.

God's Hand

The hand of God, it is not short. It is strong. It is soft and tender. It claps so tight and so firm. It does not let go but gently pulls you back…to his side. There is nothing that can compare to the love of the one who tightly grips your hand…to keep you near.

With this hand, I enter into the place of rest with my God's Son. How peaceful when holding his hand; I find my place in his kingdom. In Love I abide.

What Am I Thankful for Today?

What am I thankful for this very day?
There is the obvious:
The day, the Sunshine
The ability to breathe, the promise of spring in the air.

What about sorry? It brings repentance, am I thankful?
Rest from a wicked heart that needed to be set right?
The tears, and surely in all that, comfort from God.

And in the face of it all,
how about a friend that makes you laugh?
Or a melody on an untuned piano?
What am I thankful for today?

DEAR LORD,

Last night, I went through dread and discouragement; what was thrown in my face? Now I ask you bury it. *Or,* if it is the well of bitterness, please heal it. Let it water the pasture, that bitterness and disappointment, and may it be turned to pastures of green, where the flock eats and rests.

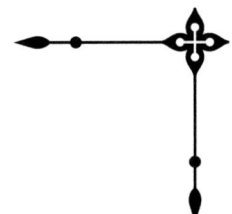

Willingness

What if the oil for the lamp is willingness?
Willingness to forgive,
Willingness to put some action away that just feeds
the flesh, Willingness to pray instead of play,
Willingness to be in God's presence with his son Jesus,
Willingness to turn away from the joys and
pleasures of the world that only decay,
Willingness to learn the Truth of God every day,
Willingness to learn of the seven spirits that search the world
for the hidden treasure of heaven in the hearts of men.

❧

Andrew (not the disciple in the Bible), if you leave the bread on
the table and do not eat it—you will starve to death.

Reflections:

_____
_____
_____
_____
_____
_____
_____

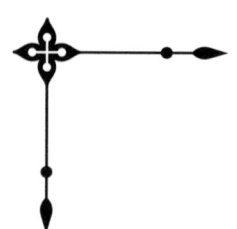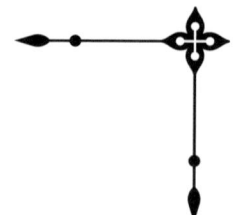

Cuddly

I have a very favorite friend, age it has no bearing in.
She has the sweetest smile and grin, with hugs galore.
My smiley friend

She always comes with wisdom, wise, she
does not this world despise.
She keeps me walking in God's path, together
we walk our hands are clasped.
My traveling friend

Her home she always has a place, where
I can rest and sit a space.
Crochet, knit, or sing a song; my friend
her faith in God is strong.
My comfort friend

Even though her hair is gray, her body
stooped from many days,
The Spirit knows not boundary set, as each day she faces yet.
My constant friend

She is my friend, my dear sweet one.
When the Lord has called her home, my
heart will smile, for her I've known.
My dear friend

Forgiveness

What is forgiveness?
The perfect calm, peace where dwells the power of letting go.
How easy it is to speak swelling words of God's mercy,
Heaping coals of fire upon my enemies' head.
Where the Father brings the fire of hope, faith, love
That restores the soul of the one that I am angry
with, am hurt, and have no confidence in.

Truly this is the mercy I seek in my life.
Restoring the soul, of one whom I am angry with,
Where we can both together in green pastures lie down,
Where God feeds us with his flock in fellowship so grand.

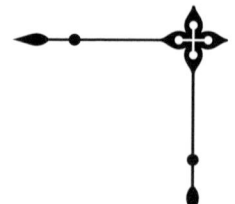

Be My Vision

Let me see up to heaven,
The wonders of a kingdom,
Where love and peace rule,
For me, through Christ Jesus,
My Lord.
My King.
The one who loves me more than love itself.

Where all is bright and beautiful,
Where being in the light is so perfect,
So satisfying that my soul drinks in the Love of
My Lord.
My King.
The one who loves me more than love itself.

One More Step

The hardest times when your soul is so desperate,
All the strength of the inward man is gone,
When everything has gone sour,
The waves of life keep rolling on; RELENTLESS
The promise of God hard on your heart,
as the flesh and the devil try to take them away.
But in all is the thought, the whisper, "I am near,"
Though at the bottom, the Lord you feel,
His Power, His Strength, and Faith revealed.
There is nothing in me to keep going on,
But the Lord, he beckons, he calls.
"One more step, please kneel in Prayer.
Listen for me, my voice you'll hear."
He calls, He whispers, hope for the day,
"My promise is sure and patience it takes,
So learn of Me.
You know I Am near,
Learn about the Love, Learn of the steps,
That brings you to ME."

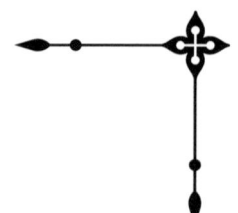

Prayer for me

I sat today, my thoughts above
Within the heavenly realm of Love,
And then without a thought of you,
My heart, it smiled, it cooed like a dove.

For that is when an upward scent,
A scent that soothes the soul.
It drifted up and filled my heart,
With joy and love ne'er told.

It was a prayer for me, it was!
Rising up from earth to heaven.
And now I know you pray for me,
A heavenly prayer toward eternity.

Thank you, dear Father, for showing me
The things that are unseen.
We take for granted every day,
Our love down here shared with thee.

Fruit Trees

I was walking down the road. There were rows of
blossoming fruit trees on both sides, trees and trees.
Beautiful they were, blossoms boldly
faced the sky drinking the sun.
So perfect! I thought until I saw three trees amongst all these
with bees and bees buzzing in the blossoms of the trees.

Why oh why are there no bees for all
the other trees? Only these?
Were those trees fake? Do they deceive?
Are these for looks? No life in these?
Are they just for today, no promise for beyond?

They cumber the ground but no fruit will be found?
Not even the bees that bring promise of the fruit
Are not drawn to these trees.
These trees have no use.
Is my life like one, that the bees they are there?
Or am I a ornament for the world to stare?
We think it's great to deceive, beauty of life to steal,
But the bees they know the fake from the real.

Without the fruit, what will the trees produce?
When the Lord comes, what will he see?
Will he find fruit in his expectancy?
Or will he say, "I never knew you, please leave me."

Where is my joy, peace, and love?
If they do not come from heaven above?
The treasure of life, in thee I have found.
Please, Dear Lord, let the fruit of the spirit abound.

❧

So what is the nature of the Spirit? Like the bee that is drawn to the sweet scent of the blossoms in the air, what draws the Spirit? If appearance is dead, it has to be life within. The seed, the blossom, the soul.

If life is preserved by staying where God has put us, then why are we so taken up with having in our life things that are dead?

A little bird singing its song in the light of the day—a joy to the sun, earth, and trees. But we complain because it pecks at the trees. A little bird to share a bite, it does not hurt the fruit but lets us know everything is all right.

We dislike bugs, like the spider who weaves her nest in kings' palaces. So quiet but menacing, bringing terror to those who see where it dwells. It is killed, smashed, swept away; without a care of those who cannot share. Oh yes, I am guilty, I have to say, of an idle word that whisks away those who struggle the kingdom to enter in. They are destroyed because of ignorance, the lack of faith in the God, Creator of heaven and earth, who knows all things.

You fill my life with good, like a tree with sweet scents and the promise of life, the bees buzzing ever so softly around and around. Please let your Spirit in me dwell: alive, in peace, in love, in hope.

Let my dreams be your dreams, for mine are not in heaven like yours. The dreams of the flesh leave me in want. But the dreams of my Lord, my Groom—yes, my Savior—are in contentment and reside in heaven.

Thank you for strength and for peace that comes from the scent of your Spirit in my life. Like a tree full of bees, let the scent of heaven call me to God's throne.

The Tree in the Vineyard

When we repent, we rest from our sin
God's work, it now truly begins.
He digs round our roots
The problem to solve.
He feeds us and prunes us,
All work is involved.

So why is it so hard
To lay down our sin?
While we sit, rest, and watch,
As our Lord he digs in.
Seems kind of crazy,
How God's work begins.

When we rest at his feet
And lay down our sin.

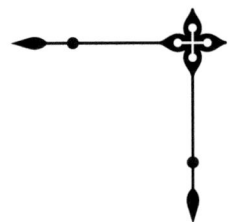

Noisy

Here I sit, life once more all in God's hand. I'm watching my brother's dogs, sitting in his house, listening to the hymns being played. They are so calming to the soul. Sitting in someone's life that does not belong to me. My little life, so fragile; a blast of wind could end it today. Somewhere is God, his Son Jesus, and the Comforter. They are ever present to sit with me.

They are quite today; I am noisy. God does not butt into conversations; he waits until he is invited. In all my days of walking with God (and that by my definition), I have not learned to listen. It still has to come about in my life to learn how to shut up and be quiet.

The elderly of God's servants are so quiet. You need to just shut up, and after a while, they may speak—some wonderful thing that will encourage, edify, or be an admonition from the Spirit of God.

There is very little quiet in the raging storm. There was very little quiet in the screaming and crying of Legion's soul. There was nothing calm about those who bound him with chains and fetters. Yet in the Lord's hand, he was found in his right mind, clothed, sitting next to Jesus. Where the conversation was quiet and soft.

I long to, need to, learn more of this quiet in my life.

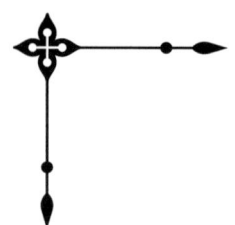

Trust Me

Can I trust you?
Who asks me to walk upright.
If it was not for you,
I would lie down and die!
In the deepest darkest night.

Your love is so complete, so safe,
It will not take me out of eternity.
To be wrapped in your arms
And smothered in your chest.

So trust you, Lord?
You are my hope, my soul's deep sigh.
I trust you. Till my life be spent.
You are my soul's great delight,
And in my heart, a very bright light.

As I Walk in the Heart of God

The Bride and the Groom

My Lord and God, the Father of my soul,
The one who Unites me with his son the groom,
Who has given me the wedding garment,
Who has adorned my soul with precious
gifts of peace and love,
Joy, Meekness, Gentleness

The one who walks with me,
Who gives me to be united forever.
To his Son,
A union of one
Lord, I long for the time,
When the business of the day
Will only be with thee.

Robert's Letter

Robby would call on the phone and sing, "I just called to say I love you". The address he wrote on the outside of the envelope. It is written on a mothers day card. I would like to think this journey of mine helped my son.

I just wrote to say, "I Love YOU"

MOM

In Jesus' hands is where I lie, don't cry for me, let your soul rest knowing I sit with God, and he held my hand that welcomed me to the promised land.

I am happy now. -Bert-
Love you mom, forever.
I'm in heaven waiting for you to come home one day too. I miss you.

Bobby.

Am I Begging at the Gate?

The dogs licked his wounds.
Where did they come from?
A rock, was it thrown?
A thoughtless word?
Or struggles from the path he walked?
And there he was found,
Begging for bread.

Was it choices for God
That left him there?
His abundance, was it Mercy from the people of God?
What a portion from the Lord to show his care,
A privilege to labor: in faith, in belief, in Love
In exchange
For a time when the beggar was wrapped
in the Father's arms.

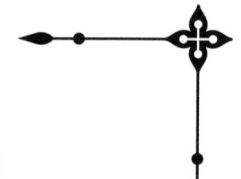

Wait on the Lord

What can I do today to serve the Lord?
What, LORD, would you have me to do?
Encourage?
Read?
Pray?
Seek thy presence?
May I bring bread?
May I bring balm?
Is there someplace NO ONE wants,
That I can fill, to do your will here on earth.
That I could fill?

As I Walk in the Heart of God

SACRED REFLECTIONS

_____

_____

_____

_____

_____

_____

_____

_____

_____

_____

_____

_____

_____

_____

_____

_____

As I Walk in the Heart of God

About the Author

Terry Lee was born in the '50s. She always states that she grew up in the whiplash of the '60s. She currently lives in Delta, Colorado, where she is amazed by the many different churches she sees. Her life had been torn apart by divorce, and the homelife with her parents was stormy at best. After her first two children were born, her hand reached for heaven, looking for God. She is now the mother of five children; four are living. As her children were growing up, they always read their Bible on Saturday night as a family, planting seeds of God in their heart. Terry Lee loves the seed and Sower. Her poems and thoughts reflect the seed God has planted in her heart. May you enjoy the messages God gave to her.

Printed by Libri Plureos GmbH in Hamburg, Germany

9 798896 831495